Genésio José da Silva
Maria Luiza da C. Santos

Research Ethics Committee

Genésio José da Silva
Maria Luiza da C. Santos

Research Ethics Committee

Contributions to the construction and development of scientific knowledge at IFPB

ScienciaScripts

Cover image: www.ingimage.com

This book is a translation from the original published under ISBN 978-3-330-76865-9.

Publisher:
Sciencia Scripts
is a trademark of
Dodo Books Indian Ocean Ltd. and OmniScriptum S.R.L publishing group

120 High Road, East Finchley, London, N2 9ED, United Kingdom
Str. Armeneasca 28/1, office 1, Chisinau MD-2012, Republic of Moldova, Europe
Managing Directors: Ieva Konstantinova, Victoria Ursu
info@omniscriptum.com

Printed at: see last page
ISBN: 978-620-8-60029-7

SUMMARY

I dedicate this work to my parents, JOSÉ MANOEL and RITA MARIA, the basis of all my education and a source of unconditional support.

Genésio José da Silva

I dedicate it to all the researchers whose studies have defined the foundations of the human dimension, especially in the context of work.

Maria Luiza da C. Santos

1 INTRODUCTION

Research ethics committees (RECs) are interdisciplinary and independent collegiate bodies with public relevance and an advisory, deliberative and educational nature. The reason for CEP's existence is to defend the interests of research participants and contribute to the development of studies within ethical standards (BRASIL, 2012).

According to Resolution 196/1996 (VII.1) of the National Health Council (CNS), institutions that carry out research involving human beings must set up one or more research ethics committees, according to their needs (BRASIL, 1996).

In 2012, the National Health Council published Resolution 466/2012, which revoked Resolution 196/96. This new regulation maintained the requirement for institutions carrying out research involving human beings to set up a research ethics committee.

Also according to Resolution 466/2012 (VII.1), research involving human beings must be submitted for appraisal to the system made up of research ethics committees and the National Research Ethics Commission, known as the CEP/CONEP system (BRASIL, 2012).

With this in mind, the Research Ethics Committee of the Federal Institute of Education, Science and Technology of Paraiba (CEP/IFPB) was created in 2008. Its mission is to ensure the rights of research participants and contribute to the development of research within ethical standards at the institution.

The IFPB currently[1] has 52 (fifty-two) courses at the secondary technical level (integrated and subsequent to secondary education), 33 (thirty-three) higher education courses, 5 (five) *lato sensu postgraduate courses and* 1 (one) *stricto sensu* postgraduate course.

Numerous research projects are carried out in the above-mentioned courses and their projects are supported by the National Council for Scientific and Technological

1 Data obtained on February 13, 2015. In the information on secondary technical courses and higher education courses, only the courses offered for entry in 2015 were taken into account. This data was obtained from the Dean of Education (PRE/IFPB). Information on *lato sensu* and *stricto sensu* postgraduate courses was obtained from the Dean of Research, Innovation and Postgraduate Studies (PRPIPG/IFPB).

Development (CNPQ), through scientific initiation and technological development and innovation scholarship programs. The IFPB, for its part, also fosters its research activities through grant programs for research staff and scientific and technological initiation programs for students. There are also projects that are carried out on a voluntary basis and others that are aimed at developing monographs at undergraduate and postgraduate level.

Research involving human beings must be submitted to the Institution's Research Ethics Committee, whose purpose is to protect study participants and contribute to the development of research in accordance with ethical standards at IFPB.

With this in mind, the IFPB's institutional calls for research grants require that, as a prerequisite for the registration of projects involving human beings, the research project be sent to the CEP by the deadline for registration, and that, as a prerequisite for receiving grants, if the project is awarded, the consubstantiated approval opinion issued by the Research Ethics Committee.

According to the above, it can be seen that the CEP/IFPB plays an important role in the institution, safeguarding the rights of research participants and contributing to the ethical quality of research carried out on the institute's various campuses.

Despite the important role played by the Research Ethics Committee, the IFPB does not currently have a study on the importance of the CEP in the construction and development of scientific knowledge at the institution, covering aspects such as: the history of the CEP/IFPB, general operating conditions and trends, and systematized data on the research protocols examined.

The relevance of this book lies in the development of a work whose results can be used by the management of the IFPB Research Ethics Committee as a subsidy to improve its activities, thus contributing to a better performance of the CEP in improving the ethical quality of the research carried out at the Institution and, consequently, to greater protection for the research participant.

Given this context, the main objective of this book is to analyze the importance of the

Research Ethics Committee in the construction and development of scientific knowledge at IFPB. Specifically, the aim was to describe the history of the CEP/IFPB in terms of its origins, founding and evolution; to verify the general operating conditions and trends of the CEP/IFPB; to characterize the research protocols examined by the CEP/IFPB, according to: area of knowledge, professional category, researchers' degrees, number per researcher and campus of origin, in the period from 2010 to 2014; and to list the number of research protocols appraised by the CEP/IFPB, according to the opinions "pending", "approved", "not approved", as well as those were "withdrawn" or "archived", in the period from 2010 to 2014.

This book has 4 (four) chapters. The first presents the introduction, contextualizing the subject covered in the book and explaining the objectives of the work. The second covers theoretical aspects related to research ethics committees. The third section analyzes the CEP/IFPB, presenting its origin and foundation, general operating conditions and trends, as well as various characteristics of the research protocols examined between 2010 and 2014. The fourth and final chapter presents the final considerations of the work, setting out the conclusions reached in the development of the work.

2 RESEARCH ETHICS COMMITTEES

Over the centuries, *there have been* reports of research involving human beings that was carried out with disrespect, humiliation, torture and death. According to Vieira and Hossne (1995), in this context, the need arose to create control mechanisms for this research, especially when the abusive scientific experiments committed in the concentration camps during the Second World War became known.

With the emergence of bioethics in the 20th century, the duty of ethical obligations towards all living beings became clear, and from the 1970s onwards there was a greater concern with bioethics applied to research involving human beings.

If, on the one hand, abusive research with human beings contributed to the emergence of research ethics committees, on the other, bioethics served to strengthen them, through its principles and proposition of ethical obligations in the practice of scientific research with human beings.

2.1 HISTORY OF RESEARCH INVOLVING HUMAN BEINGS

Over the centuries, there have been countless reports of situations in which ethical elements were disregarded in the production of scientific knowledge, abusive situations involving human beings. Several examples of the inappropriate use of people in research have been recorded, facts that deserve reflection and should not be repeated (ARAÙJO, 2012).

In Alexandria, in the third century BC, Herophilus and Erasistratus made great anatomical and physiological discoveries. Herophilus, considered the founder of anatomy, made precise descriptions of the brain, differentiated tendons from nerves, distinguished between arteries, veins and capillaries and studied the eye extensively. Erasistratus, considered the "father of physiology", created comparative and pathological anatomy, discovered that all organs were connected to the triple system formed by arteries, veins and nerves and proved that arteries contained only pneuma, and that veins contained blood. Both Herophilus and Erasistratus practiced the vivisection of human beings, usually criminals, dissecting them alive, with the king's permission and observing (while they were still breathing) all the hidden parts of the body (VRETTOS, 2005).

In 1559, at the height of the Renaissance, the king of France, Henry II, had his eye and right temple pierced by a spear during a competition. The king was treated by the surgeon Ambròsio Paré and the anatomist André Vesàlio. In order to find a remedy for her husband's wound, Queen Catherine de Medici ordered criminals to be beheaded so that, by inserting rods into their right eye, doctors could correctly determine the extent of the king's injury (READING, 2012).

In 1796, the English doctor Edmund Jenner, in his quest to find a method of preventing variola, conducted his studies with vaccines that were used on his children and neighboring children, putting them at risk and without worrying about their protection (KIPPER, 2010). According to Diniz and Guilhem (2005), Jenner went further in his research, including prisoners and abandoned children as research subjects, making the vulnerability of the study participants evident.

In the 19th century, the American doctor William Beaumont, considered to be the founder of Gastroenterology, carried out an ethically questionable study. The study was carried out on the patient Alexis St. Martin, who had a sequela in his abdomen caused by a gunshot wound, which made it possible to observe the inside of his stomach. In this research, the doctor signed a documented agreement with the research subject, in which he would be available for all the experiments that were carried out, for a period of one year. In return, the patient would receive a certain amount of money for their participation, as well as food and shelter (MINOSSI, 2011).

Still in the 19th century, in 1900, a commission of US Army doctors was sent to Cuba to study the natural history of yellow fever. During the study, American soldiers were exposed to mosquitoes that transmitted the disease (ARAÙJO, 2012).

Between 1932 and 1945, Japan waged destructive biological warfare in some Asian countries. China, Korea and the Manchurian region were the main stage for research aimed at developing biological weapons. According to Martins (2006), Japanese researchers wrote the most terrible pages in the entire history of the medical profession, laboratory biomedicine and experiments on human beings, breaking all the moral barriers of scientific research. During this period, thousands of human beings, civilians and prisoners of war, were used as involuntary guinea pigs and subjected to unrestricted experiments. According to the author, in the name of "research and development" of increasingly powerful biological weapons, Japanese researchers carried out vivisections on living human beings (including pregnant women and babies) and spread, from their laboratories, a variety of diseases such as bubonic plague, typhus, paratyphoid, syphilis, cholera, diphtheria, yellow fever, bacterial and viral meningitis, viral pneumonia, variola, hantavirus disease, *anthrax*, etc.

From 1932 to 1972, at the health center in the city of Tuskegee, Alabama, United States (USA), a study was carried out with the aim of observing the natural evolution of syphilis without any treatment. The study was conducted by the US Public Health Service and involved the participation of 600 (six hundred) black men, of whom 399 (three hundred and ninety-nine) were infected with Syphilis and 201 (two hundred and one) without the disease. According to Goldim (1999), the research participants were not informed that they had syphilis or of its effects. For taking part in the study, they received meals, some cash prizes, medical care and funeral assistance. According to the author, even with the emergence of a treatment for syphilis in the 1950s, the participants were kept without medication. The Tuskegee case gained strong social and political repercussions in 1972, when the *New York Times* published a story denouncing the project. After this repercussion, the study was terminated, leaving only 74 (seventy-four) survivors of the infected participants.

In Germany, during the Second World War (1939 - 1945), Nazi doctors carried out inhumane and cruel experiments on human beings. The atrocities committed during this period in the name of science had no ethical limits. Araùjo (2012, p. 73) highlights the repercussions of Nazi experiments on the history of research involving human beings:

> Of all the historical events involving research with human beings, those that have had the most negative repercussions relate to the atrocities committed by Nazi doctors during the Second World War in the concentration camps in Germany, which became veritable laboratories for scientific experimentation on

humans.

In the Nazi concentration camps, research was carried out to investigate the treatment of malaria. In these experiments, prisoners were infected by the mosquito that caused the disease and then treated with various drugs to test their effectiveness. The Nazi experiments also included exposing human beings to gases that caused severe chemical burns, with the aim of then finding the best treatment for the burns (CARBONIERI, 2013).

Approximately 300 prisoners of war were subjected to freezing experiments in the Dachau concentration camp. The purpose of the study was to find the most efficient heating technique for the German army, which was facing the European winter. In these experiments, the prisoners screamed in pain as part of their bodies were frozen at a temperature below zero degrees Celsius for several hours (VIEIRA, 2005).

In Auschwitz, with the aim of investigating some genetic characteristics, the Nazi doctor Mengele subjected 1,500 pairs of twins to his experiments, leaving a catastrophic balance of less than 200 (two hundred) survivors (GUERRA, 2006). The atrocities committed by the Nazis did not all go unpunished. Criminals from the Second World War were tried, including some doctors who took part in the murders and torture in the concentration camps. According to Costa (2008, p. 28), "The perversity of the accounts during the Nuremberg Trials was decisive in the conviction of Nazi doctors and scientists for war crimes and crimes against humanity." In this context, the first code of ethics for research involving human beings was created:

> Out of the horrors revealed in these trials came the Nuremberg Code, which also represents a historical break. Although this document was triggered by the events revealed, it does not refer to them, but to the conduct that a scientific researcher should follow. It is a demonstration of wisdom that this first code of research ethics avoided alluding to highly anomalous situations and preferred to focus on general ethical norms valid for all research. Even so, the fact that a trial of war criminals inspired a code of research ethics is striking (KOTTOW, 2008, p.61).

Despite having spelled out a set of ethical precepts that should be applied in research involving human beings, the Nuremberg Code, during its first twenty years of existence, failed to achieve its true objective. In the United States, perverse and abusive experiments with vulnerable participants were widely developed in the 1960s and 1970s (DINIZ; CORRÊA, 2001).

In 1963, in an Israeli hospital for chronic diseases in New York, elderly patients, unaware of the actual procedure of the study they were undergoing, were injected with live cancer cells. The experiment aimed to study the body's defense mechanisms (COSTA, 2008). Also in New York, between 1950 and 1970, mentally handicapped children admitted to Willowbrook Public Hospital were infected with the hepatitis virus. The experiment was aimed at finding a vaccine for the disease (BOCCATO, 2007).

The Nuremberg Code was revised in 1964 at the 18ª Assembly of the World Medical Association, which also approved the Declaration of Helsinki, which established the need for research protocols to be reviewed by an independent committee. This Declaration was revised in the 70s, 80s and 90s (FREITAS, HOSSNE, 1998).

The cases reported in the previous examples constitute unethical conduct in the process of producing scientific knowledge. They demonstrate practices that should not be followed in research and serve as a reflection so that atrocities disguised as scientific progress are no longer committed against human beings.

2.2 ORIGINS AND EVOLUTION OF BIOETHICS IN THE INTERNATIONAL CONTEXT

The forerunner of bioethics[2] was the German Albert Schweitzer, who in 1923 founded bioethical thinking in the text *Ethics of Reverence for Life*[3] . Schweitzer's text was responsible for later influencing authors such as Jahr, Leopold and Potter (CARVALHO; PESSINI, CAMPOS JÙNIOR, 2006).

In 1927, the word bioethics was used for the first time, when Fritz Jahr published an article in the German periodical *Kosmos.* The author characterized bioethics as the recognition of ethical obligations, not just towards man, but towards all living beings

2 A neologism constructed from the Greek words *bios* (life)+ *ethos* (ethics).
3 *Ethics of reverence for life.*

(GOLDIM, 2006).

In 1949, the American Aldo Leopold broadened the concept of bioethics proposed by Jahr to include, in addition to plants and animals, the soil and other natural resources from the point of view of ethical reflection (FUENTES, 2011).

From the 1970s onwards, the neologism bioethics became popular with the publication of the book Bioethics*: bridge to the* future by the American biologist and oncologist Van Rensselaer Potter (OLIVEIRA, 1997 apud OLIVEIRA, 2007). According to Garrafa (2010), Potter envisioned bioethics as a macroethics, related to human life in a broader way, encompassing not only biomedical and biotechnological issues, but also linked to environmental issues and the sustainability of the planet.

In 1971, obstetrician André Hellegers founded the *Joseph and Rose Kennedy Institute for the Study of Human Reproduction and Bioethics,* which became known as the Kennedy Institute of Ethics. Due to the technological advances in the health area, Hellegers, unlike Potter, considered bioethics in a microbiological sense, focusing essentially on the clinical side, mainly on the applications of biology and medicine in human life (AZEVEDO, 2010).

Three notable cases were responsible for the emergence of principialist bioethics in the US in the 1970s: the study of people with syphilis in Tuskegee; the experiments carried out on the elderly at the Israeli hospital in New York; and those carried out on children at Willowbrook. These episodes mobilized US public opinion and demanded ethical regulation (PESSINI; BARCHIFONTAINE, 2007). According to these authors:

> Reacting to these scandals, the US government, via Congress, set up the National Commission for the Protection of Human Subjects *of* Biomedical and Behavioral Research in 1974, with the aim of *"carrying out a comprehensive survey and study that would identify the basic ethical principles that should guide human experimentation in the behavioral sciences and biomedicine"* (PESSINI; BARCHIFONTAINE, 2007, p. 56).

The result of the commission's work was published four years later (1978) and became known as the Belmont Report. This report presented three basic ethical principles for research involving human beings: respect for persons, beneficence and justice (COSTA, 2008).

In 1979, Tom Beauchamp and James Childress published a work[4] in which they added the principle of non-maleficence to those already set out in the Belmont Report (CASCAIS, 2006). According to Dejeanne (2011, p. 3) "the academic consolidation of bioethics was confirmed with the theoretical proposal of Beauchamp and Childress, the first to systematize the basic principles [...] in the field of biomedical action".

In the 1980s, bioethics expanded and consolidated itself on all continents through events, books and specialized scientific journals, mainly based on the principialist theory of Beauchamp and Childress (GARRAFA, 2005).

2.3 BIOETHICS IN BRAZIL

The first official Brazilian document aimed at regulating research in the health area was Resolution No·01/88 of the National Health Council (CNS) (MARQUES FILHO, 2007). According to Marques (2009, p. 1) "This resolution establishes levels of risk and provides normative guidelines for good ethical conduct and safety, to be observed in health research conducted in the national territory and involving human beings".

In 1991, the book *Problemas atuais de bioética* was published, the first Brazilian book on the subject, written by Father Léo Pessini and nurse Christian de Paul de Barchifontaine (DALL'AGNOL, 2012).

In 1993, the journal Bioética was created in Brasilia, sponsored by the Federal Council of Medicine (GARRAFA, 2000). According to Oliveira (2008), the first two years of the magazine covered subjects that consisted of a reflection on the health problems inherent in controversial issues linked to patient autonomy and the taboos of Brazilian society.

In 1995, the Brazilian Society of Bioethics (SBB) was officially founded, with William Saad Hossne as its first president (HOSSNE *et al*, 2010). According to Pessini and Barchifontaine (2007), the SBB emerged informally in 1992 at the Universidade Estadual Paulista Júlio de Mesquita Filho (UNESP) in Botucatu (SP) under the leadership of Professor Hossne. According to the authors, the SBB has the following

4 *Principles of Biomedical Ethics*

aims:

1) bring together people from different scientific or humanistic backgrounds interested in promoting the progress and dissemination of bioethics; 2) stimulate the cultural production of its members and disseminate the purposes of bioethics; 3) advise, when requested, on projects and activities in the field of bioethics; 4) support movements and activities aimed at enhancing bioethics and participate in them (PESSINI; BARCHIFONTAINE, 2007, p. 17).

Also in 1995, the National Health Council began a process of reviewing CNS Resolution 01/88 with the aim of updating it. As a result, an Executive Working Group (GET) was set up, made up of representatives from various social and professional areas, resulting in the drafting of CNS Resolution 196/96 (FREITAS; HOSSNE, 1998). Guilhem and Diniz (2005, p. 18) demonstrate the importance of Resolution 196/96 in the Brazilian context:

This document can be considered a milestone for the research scene in Brazil. The proposed norms and guidelines take into account contemporary technical and scientific advances and are strongly aligned with the bioethical principles of autonomy, beneficence, non-maleficence and justice, which have been widely used in the context of research practice internationally. In addition to these, other principles are contained at the heart of the resolution, including confidentiality, privacy, voluntariness, equity and non-stigmatization. These precepts function as an additional safeguard for the protection of the subjects taking part, and also aim to guarantee the rights and duties of scientists, sponsors, the institutions involved, the state and the subjects themselves.

Resolution 196/96 was also responsible for the creation of the CEP/CONEP System, a national system for the ethical evaluation of research involving human beings, made up of the National Research Ethics Commission and the research ethics committees (NOVAES; GUILHEM; LOLAS, 2008). According to Diniz and Guilhem (2005, p. 18) "Unlike the previous resolution, which focused on biomedical or health research, the new resolution was more comprehensive, including research involving human beings in all areas of knowledge".

In 2002, the **VI World Congress of Bioethics** was held in Brasilia. The event was organized by the Brazilian Society of Bioethics, the International Association of Bioethics and a range of institutions, public and community universities. Considered the largest congress in the field in terms of participation, the event had 1352 (one thousand three hundred and fifty-two) participants, 900 (nine hundred) Brazilians and

452 (four hundred and fifty-two) foreigners from 62 (sixty) countries. With the theme of **bioethics, power and injustice,** the event was responsible for etching into the history of bioethics worldwide issues inherent in the socio-politics of exclusion and injustice in the poor and developing world (PESSINI, HOSSNE, 2012).

In 2013, after almost 17 (seventeen) years in force in our country, CNS Resolution 196/1996 was revoked by CNS Resolution 466/2012. The new document, which also establishes guidelines and regulatory standards for research involving human beings at the national level, came into force on June 13, 2013, the date of its publication in the Official Gazette of the Union (DOU). According to Laureano (2013), Resolution 466/12 brought innovations to the content of the standard, broadening the ethical aspects of research involving human beings and considering the Informed Consent Form (ICF) as a "process".

From CNS Resolution No·01/88 to the present day, bioethics has been gradually gaining ground in Brazil. The number of books published on the subject, the number of events on the subject and the standardization of this field of study, mainly through resolutions issued by the National Health Council, are growing in our country.

2.4 RESEARCH ETHICS COMMITTEES IN BRAZIL AND PARAiBA

In Brazil, the ethical review system for research involving human beings was created by CNS Resolution 01/1988 (BATISTA *et al*, 2012). According to this document:

> Art. 83 - In every health institution accredited by the National Health Council in which research is carried out, there must be: I. ETHICS COMMITTEE if research is carried out on human beings; II. BIOLOGICAL SAFETY COMMITTEE if research is carried out that involves the use of devices that generate ionizing and electromagnetic radiation, radioactive isotopes, pathogenic microorganisms, recombinant nucleic acids or other analogous procedures that may pose a risk to health (BRASIL, 1988).

In 1996, Resolution 01/88 underwent a revision process, giving rise to CNS Resolution 196/96. The new document stipulates that all research involving human beings, not just biomedical research, must be approved by a research ethics committee (HARDY *et al*, 2004). In addition, Resolution 196/96 provides for the establishment of RECs in institutions that carry out research involving human beings:

VIII.1 - Institutions which carry out research involving human beings must set up one or more Research Ethics Committees (RECs), depending on their needs. **VIII.2** - If it is not possible to set up a REC, the institution or the researcher responsible must submit the project for appraisal by another institution's REC, necessarily among those indicated by the National Research Ethics Committee (CONEP/MS) (BRASIL, 1996).

It is important to note that all the costs inherent in setting up and running the REC are borne by the institution, so institutional engagement is an indispensable condition for setting up and running the committee (BATISTA *et al*, 2012). It is also worth noting that after its creation, in order for the REC to be authorized to function, the institution must apply to CONEP for registration and accreditation of the committee. According to Batista *et al* (2012), the request must contain the following documents: the act creating the research ethics committee; details of the requesting institution, describing its mission and activities; details of the members of the committee's collegiate body, the coordinator and the user representative and the minimum conditions for the CEP to function.

Once the CEP has been registered and accredited by CONEP, the research ethics committee is entitled to carry out the ethical assessment of research protocols involving human beings. However, the performance of its activities does not only require legitimacy. According to Freitas and Hossne (1998), in addition to legitimacy, the CEP's work also depends on adequate infrastructure, which includes a prepared team, operational and organizational facilities and a budget.

After almost 17 (seventeen) years in force in our country, in 2013 Resolution 196 was revoked by Resolution 466/2012. According to this Resolution (VII.2) the RECs are:

[...] interdisciplinary and independent collegiate bodies, of public relevance, of an advisory, deliberative and educational nature, created to defend the interests of research participants in their integrity and dignity and to contribute to the development of research within ethical standards (BRASIL, 2012).

Resolution 466/12 provides for the following duties for research ethics committees:

VIII.1 - evaluate research protocols involving human beings, with priority given to issues of public relevance and strategic interest on the SUS agenda of priorities, based on epidemiological indicators, issuing an opinion, duly justified, always guided, among others, by the principles of impersonality, transparency, reasonableness, proportionality and efficiency, within the deadlines established in an operational standard, avoiding redundancies that result in delays in the analysis; VIII.2 - play an advisory and educational role in matters of ethics; and VIII.3 - draw up its Internal Regulations (BRASIL, 2012).

In addition to evaluating research protocols, the CEP is also responsible for monitoring the study, either through six-monthly reports or other means of monitoring depending on the risk of the research (BRASIL, 2012).

As for its educational role, according to the Operational Manual for Research Ethics Committees, the CEP should promote the initial training and ongoing training of its members, researchers and research participants, and should also promote discussion on the ethical aspects of research involving human beings in the community (BRASIL, 2008).

Also in 2013, the National Health Council published Operational Standard 001/2013, which regulates the procedural and administrative aspects of the CEP/CONEP system. According to this document, research ethics committees must have a minimum of 7 (seven) members, including at least 1 (one) user representative. Its members must have a degree in various fields of knowledge, at least 50% must have experience in research and must include participants of both sexes. It can also count on "ad hoc" consultants (BRASIL, 2013).

As for the procedure for submitting a research protocol for ethical review by the CEP/CONEP System, according to Operational Standard 001/2013, the researcher responsible must be previously registered on the Brazil Platform[5] , as only research protocols launched on this system will be considered, and must have all the necessary documentation in Portuguese, accompanied by the originals, if any (BRASIL, 2013). According to Batista *et al* (2012), the implementation of the Brazil Platform took place in January 2012 and aimed to cover the entire CEP/CONEP System.

It is worth noting that the submission of a research protocol to the CEP/CONEP system, as long as it involves human beings, not only does it not depend on the area of knowledge, but also on the level of the study. In this sense, according to Batista *et al* (2012, p. 151), "The submission of the protocol to a CEP is independent of the level of

5 Information system that allows researchers to submit and follow the processing of research protocols online.

the research, and can be a work for the conclusion of an undergraduate course, scientific initiation or doctorate and of academic or operational interest, as long as it falls within the definition of 'research involving human beings'".

After the submission process, through Plataforma Brasil, the research protocols arrive at the CEP secretariat, which distributes them to the members and coordinator to carry out the reporting. After the rapporteur's opinion has been analyzed and drafted, the protocols are evaluated by the other members of the committee at a monthly or fortnightly meeting, depending on the number of research protocols being processed. In order to deliberate on the protocols, more than half of the members of the committee must be present (BATISTA *et al*, 2012).

With regard to the deliberation of research protocols, the decision of the collegiate body can result in the issuance of the following opinions: pending, approved or not approved. According to CNS Resolution 466/2012 (X.3.5.b), the research protocol falls into the pending category "when the CEP considers it necessary to correct the protocol submitted, and requests specific revision, modification or relevant information, which must be met within a period stipulated in an operational rule" (BRASIL, 2012).

In addition to the categories of opinions mentioned above, research protocols can also be considered withdrawn or archived. According to CNS Resolution 466/2012, a research protocol is considered withdrawn when there is a request from the researcher responsible (BRASIL, 2012). It is worth noting that until 2011, according to CNS Resolution 196/96, in addition to the aforementioned characteristic, research protocols were also considered withdrawn when the researchers did not comment on the pending issues pointed out by the committee within 60 (sixty) days (BRASIL, 1996). However, from 2012 onwards, after the process of revising CNS Resolution 196/96, only research protocols that were requested to be withdrawn at the request of the researcher were considered withdrawn. Research protocols in which the researchers did not respond to the pending issues listed by the CEP within 60 (sixty) days are now called archived. CNS Resolution 466/2012, which revoked Resolution 196/96, maintained this same orientation, but the deadline for the researcher to comment on the pending issues listed, instead of 60 (sixty) days, was defined in an operational rule .[6]

Regarding the number of existing CEP, according to data published by CONEP, in September 2014, Brazil had 694 (six hundred and ninety-four) CEP as shown in figure 1, of which 49.42% are located in the Southeast, 19.60% in the Northeast, 18.44% in the South, 6.92% in the North and 5.62% in the Midwest.

Figure 1 - CEP registered with CONEP, by region and state

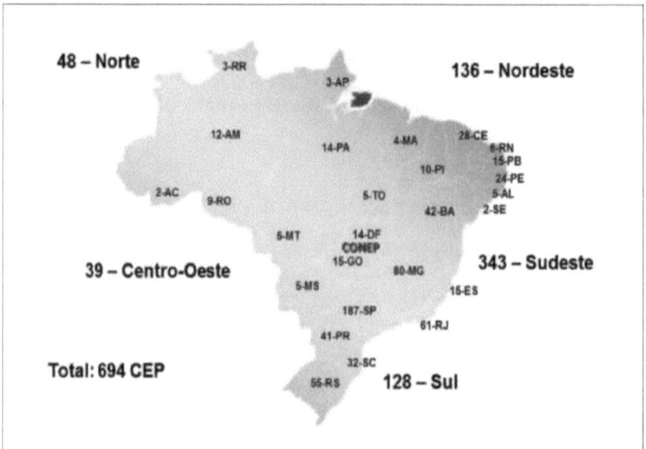

Source: CONEP website, 2014.

As for the distribution of RECs by state, Sao Paulo has the highest number: 187 (one hundred and eighty-seven), corresponding to 26.95% of the total number of research ethics committees in the country. In the Northeast, the state with the highest number of RECs is Bahia: 42 (forty-two), representing 30.88% of the region's research ethics committees. Paraiba has 15 (fifteen)RECs, corresponding to 11.03% of the total in the Northeast, ranking 4th in number of research ethics committees in the region. As shown in Table 1, Paraiba has 7 (seven) RECs linked to public institutions and 8 (eight) linked to private institutions.

Chart 1 - Research ethics committees in Paraiba

6 Operational Standard 01/2013 was issued by the National Health Council on September 30, 2013, stipulating a deadline of 30 days for the researcher responsible to respond to the pending issues listed in the opinion issued by the Research Ethics Committee through the Brazil Platform.

RESEARCH ETHICS COMMITTEES/PB	CONEP REGISTRATION
Research Ethics Committee of the Teacher Training Center - Campus of Cajazeiras of UFCG	15/10/2012
Research Ethics Committee of the Paraiba Higher Education Institute - CEP/IESP	20/08/2010
Research Ethics Committee of the Alcides Carneiro University Hospital / Federal University of Campina Grande - CEP/HUAC	20/09/2011
Faculty of Santa Maria Research Ethics Committee - CEP/FSM	13/12/2007
Research Ethics Committee of Santa Emilia de Rodat College - CEP/FASER	08/11/2002
Research Ethics Committee of the State University of Paraiba - CEP/UEPB	21/05/2002
Research Ethics Committee of the Center for Higher Education and Development - CEP/Cesed	01/09/2008
Research Ethics Committee of the Faculty of Medical Sciences of Paraiba - CEP/FCM	16/07/2009
Research Ethics Committee of the Federal Institute of Education, Science and Technology of Paraiba - CEP/IFPB	23/10/2009
Research Ethics Committee of the Health Sciences Center of the Federal University of Paraiba - CEP/CCS	08/11/2010
Human Research Ethics Committee of the Faculdades Integradas de Patos - CEP/FIP	05/12/2007
Research Ethics Committee of the University Center of Joào Pessoa - CEP/UNIPÊ	05/03/2008
Research Ethics Committee of the Paraiba State Health Department - CEP/SES/PB	23/11/2004
Research Ethics Committee of the Nova Esperança Faculties of Nursing and Medicine - CEP-CEM/FACENE/FAMENE	18/11/2005
Research Ethics Committee of the Lauro Wanderley University Hospital of the Federal University of Paraiba - CEP/HULW	03/06/1997

Source: CONEP e-mail, 2014.

It is important to note that according to table 1, the IFPB Research Ethics Committee is relatively young compared to the others, having been in existence for less than 5 (five) years. The oldest CEP in the state is the Research Ethics Committee of the Lauro

Wanderley University Hospital, of the Federal University of Paraiba - CEP/HULW.

3 IFPB RESEARCH ETHICS COMMITTEE

The IFPB Research Ethics Committee is located at Avenida Joao da Mata, 256, Jaguaribe, Joao Pessoa - PB. The CEP/IFPB was created on December 9, 2008 by Resolution 013/2008 of the Board of Directors, and its registration was approved by CONEP on October 23, 2009.

The IFPB Research Ethics Committee is an interdisciplinary and independent collegiate body, of public relevance, with an advisory, deliberative and educational nature, created to defend the interests of research participants in their integrity and dignity and to contribute to the development of research within ethical standards.

3.1 HISTORY OF THE IFPB RESEARCH ETHICS COMMITTEE

The data inherent in the history of the CEP/IFPB was extracted from interviews with two researchers who took part in the process of founding the Committee and who will be identified in this paper as respondent A and respondent B. The interviews, which took place on 24/07/2014 and 02/09/2014, aimed to describe the origin and founding of the Research Ethics Committee.

According to respondent A, in the years prior to the creation of the CEP at the Institute, IFPB researchers, when carrying out research involving human beings, had to direct their research projects to the committees of other institutions, which can be seen in her speech, described below: "From then on, I began to mobilize with the managers of the research area so that we could also have our own, because all the research I did in that period, between 2005, 2006 and 2007, I ended up going to the CEP of the Health Department. So I began to realize that we had to motivate our colleagues and our management, who still didn't have this perception, this vision or this knowledge."

This perspective is also shared by respondent B, who points out the favorable context for the creation of the CEP/IFPB: "it was born out of a need for the institution because it has been growing a lot since it became an institute, and this transformation even took place in December 2008". From respondent B's statement, it can be inferred that the expansion of the IFPB has also led to an increase in scientific research carried out at the Institute, given that research is one of the Institution's core activities. From this perspective, in order for the scientific knowledge derived from this activity to be built and developed with ethical quality, it is necessary to create a research ethics committee which, according to Resolution 466/2012 (VII.2), are collegiate bodies "created to defend the interests of research participants in their integrity and dignity and to contribute to the development of research within ethical standards (BRASIL, 2012).

Respondent B also points out that another need for the Research Ethics Committee to be set up at the institution is related to the course evaluations promoted by the Anisio Teixeira National Institute for Educational Studies and Research (INEP). According to the respondent, "another point that led us to seek the creation of the CEP was the obligation required in the recognition of degree courses. When INEP comes to evaluate these courses, it immediately looks to see if the institution is carrying out research and, if so, it must have a research ethics committee."

In addition to the points of view presented by the respondents, CNS Resolution 196/96, in force at the time the CEP/IFPB was founded, in its item VII.1, stated that "Institutions in which research involving human beings is carried out should set up one or more research ethics committees - CEP, according to their needs" (BRASIL, 1996).

For respondent A, her knowledge of the research ethics committee came from a researcher in the field of dentistry at the Federal University of Paraiba (UFPB), with whom she carried out research in partnership. This researcher was responsible for bringing experience and providing knowledge about the workings and activities of the RECs, since he was already a member of a research ethics committee at UFPB and also provided support for the workings of the Research Ethics Committee of the Paraiba State Health Department. This researcher even acted as a member of the CEP/IFPB in the first formation of the group.

Respondent A also records the prevailing conception at the time among IFPB researchers regarding research ethics committees "Most of our researchers didn't have this notion, because we are from a technical area and there is a culture that the CEP is only for the health area [...] and then when I studied the CEP, I said it's not like that, you deal with people, you have to have a research ethics committee". This thought is in line with Brazilian legislation on ethics in research involving human beings, which according to Diniz and Guilhem (2005), since CNS Resolution 196/96, has advocated that all research involving human beings, regardless of the area of knowledge to which they belong, should be submitted to a research ethics committee. This contrasts with Resolution 01/88, now revoked, which was focused only on the biomedical or health areas.

Respondent B explains the important role of the UFPB researcher and respondent A in the process of creating the CEP/IFPB: "I remember well who was in charge at the beginning of this creation [...] this need was awakened even by her [...] and she brought with her two researchers from UFPB, who also helped us a lot [...] they are from the Dentistry course".

In view of the above, it can be seen that the initial idea of creating a Research Ethics Committee at IFPB came from the initiative of a researcher at the Institution, who realized the need to create a CEP at the Institute. In this process, the support provided by a researcher from UFPB, who brought with him experiences from other committees, as well as other experienced researchers, was of fundamental importance. These factors, combined with the expansion of the institution, the system for evaluating courses by INEP and the guidelines contained in CNS Resolution 196/96, provided an extremely favorable context for the creation of the IFPB Research Ethics Committee.

According to respondent A, the idea of creating a CEP at IFPB was taken to the institution's Dean of Research, who provided all the necessary support for the Committee to be created at the Institute. Respondent B, who at the time was also involved in the management of the Dean of Research, shows how this process went: "we went maturing the idea, also trying to find out what the research ethics committee was, because it was also something new for us and then when everything was ready between us, we took the proposal to the rector, told him how the process went and he gave us his full support. Then, as the CEP is an institutional body, it had to go through the Board of Directors and it was through the rector that the process was forwarded to this collegiate body."

It can be seen from the respondents' statements that institutional support was of fundamental importance for the creation of the CEP. The information emanating from their speeches is in line with the concept of Batista *et al* (2012, p. 151) who stresses that "institutional involvement is the imperative condition for the creation and operation of the REC, as all costs will be waived by the institution".

In this context, on December 9, 2008, the CEP/IFPB was created by means of Resolution 013/2008 of the Board of Directors, a body equivalent to the Board of Governors today. The Committee's internal regulations were also approved on the same date.

After the institutional act creating the Committee was completed, all the necessary documents were sent to CONEP on May 27, 2009, so that the CEP/IFPB could be accredited and authorized to operate. In order to request accreditation for a CEP, the institution must send CONEP the following documents: the act creating the research ethics committee; details of the requesting institution, describing its mission and activities; details of the members of the committee's collegiate body, the coordinator and the user representative and the minimum conditions for the CEP to function (BATISTA *et al*, 2012).

On October 23, 2009, the Committee's registration was approved by CONEP. As of that date, CEP/IFPB was authorized to carry out the ethical assessment of research protocols involving human beings.

3.2 CEP/IFPB: GENERAL OPERATING CONDITIONS AND TRENDS

The data inherent to the general operating conditions and trends of the CEP/IFPB were extracted from an interview held on July 22, 2014 with the current coordinator of the Institution's Research Ethics Committee, identified in this paper as <u>respondent C</u>. The purpose of the interview was to ascertain the general operating conditions and trends of the Committee.

When asked when and how he was appointed coordinator of the IFPB Research Ethics

Committee, respondent C gave the following answer: "at the beginning of 2009 there was a first meeting after the members had been invited [...] and at that first meeting, as stipulated in the CEP's Internal Regulations, the coordinator had to be chosen [...] so they chose me as coordinator".

Respondent C also records how the "process of preparing the ground" for the analysis of the first research protocols took place: "Our CEP was created at the end of 2008, the commission received the ordinance at the end of February 2009 and we only obtained CONEP registration in October 2009. So we spent the whole of 2009 gathering information, reading up on the legislation, holding training meetings for the members, which is why we only started evaluating research projects in 2010. So more than a year passed between the creation of the Board of Directors and the first meeting to evaluate research projects. It was during this period that we gained knowledge and experience, including taking part in meetings at other RECs here in Joao Pessoa."

As respondents A and B pointed out, respondent C also highlights the important contributions of researchers from UFPB in the Committee's initial activities: "In the beginning we had a larger number of people from the Dentistry area, who helped us a lot at the beginning of the CEP. They were people who had already taken part in the Research Ethics Committee of the Federal University of Paraiba and who had a lot of experience, which was very useful, including for the internal training of the members."

With regard to the general operating conditions and trends of the CEP/IFPB, respondent C was asked about the following points: the CEP's physical facilities and furniture, the Committee's composition, the distribution of research protocols among the members, the dynamics of the meetings, monitoring the development of research projects, the communication process with the main stakeholders, the promotion of educational activities, the main difficulties faced and the Committee's trends.

Regarding the CEP/IFPB's physical facilities and furnishings, respondent C points out that "we have our own room, our own furniture, our own computers and restricted access to the Committee's documents [...] so in terms of physical facilities and furnishings, we're fine, but we have a small shortcoming when it comes to landlines and faxes, because since we don't have a landline, we're using a mobile phone, which is also shared with other sectors". In this sense, it can be seen that, in addition to legitimacy, the work of the research ethics committee also depends on adequate infrastructure, which includes, among other factors, operational facilities (FREITAS; HOSSNE, 1998).

Regarding the composition of the Committee, which is currently made up of 17 (seventeen) members, respondent C reports that "Among these seventeen members, we have a user representative, who was appointed by the Municipal Health Council, we also have a representative from our student body

[...] and the other members are employees of the Institute, teachers and administrative technicians in the various areas of knowledge, some with master's degrees, doctorates, other specialists and we also have an external member from the Federal University of Paraiba [...] so as far as the composition of our CEP is concerned, I believe it is quite satisfactory due to the diversity of professionals from the most diverse areas." The composition of the CEP/IFPB is in line with Araùjo (2003), who points out that research ethics committees should be multidisciplinary, made up of professionals from different areas of knowledge, and should also include the participation of a user representative.

With regard to the criteria used to distribute research protocols among the members, respondent C points out that research protocols are currently received via the Brazil Platform. Initially, a documentary analysis is carried out by the CEP Secretariat to check that the necessary documentation is in order. If the documentation does not meet the minimum conditions to be forwarded to the rapporteur, it will be returned to the researcher responsible to make adjustments. If the documentation meets the standards for acceptance, the project is forwarded to a rapporteur, as can be seen from respondent C: "we try to direct the research protocol to the member whose profile is closest to the subject of the project, however, we also look at the number of protocols that each member receives, so as not to overload some and leave others unanalyzed [...] we also look at the experience of the member, due to the complexity of some research protocols, but this is not the determining factor".

Regarding the dynamics of the Committee's meetings, respondent C said that the meetings are held in a closed room, and only members and the CEP secretary are allowed access. The research protocols being processed are analyzed using the Brazil Platform, whose image is projected onto a screen using a multimedia projector, making it possible for all members to follow along.

According to respondent C, the quorum for deliberations on research protocols is initially verified, with a minimum of more than half of the members, i.e. nine members. If there is no quorum for deliberations on research protocols, general matters of interest to the Research Ethics Committee are discussed. If there is a quorum, information and/or requests from the internal research community and/or CONEP are passed on to the members of the CEP collegiate body, among other matters. The coordinator of the Research Ethics Committee then gives the floor to a rapporteur member who has been previously appointed to report on a particular research protocol. The rapporteur presents his report, usually reading out his opinion. After this procedure, a space is opened up for discussion, questions or comments regarding the research protocol that has been reported on, and then, by consensus, a decision is made on whether the protocol is pending, approved or not approved. Respondent C also points out that the events of the meeting are recorded in the minutes. This information from respondent C is in line with Batista *et al* (2012, p. 151) who states:

> After the rapporteur has drawn up his opinion, the projects are forwarded to the other members of the CEP for evaluation at monthly or fortnightly meetings, depending on the number of projects to be analyzed. Meetings must be attended by more than half of the collegiate body in order to deliberate and/or approve research projects and must be recorded in the minutes, signed by all those present.

With regard to the process of monitoring the development of research projects, respondent C said that "Although it's not ideal, we are monitoring it by requesting reports, we are demanding the final report after the project is finished and we will now also demand a partial report, especially for research that has been carried out for a year or more". Although the CEP/IFPB monitors research through reports, it does not use other means of monitoring, because according to CNS Resolution 466/12, it is the

CEP's responsibility, in addition to monitoring the development of projects through six-monthly reports, to use other monitoring strategies depending on the risk of the research (BRASIL, 2012). Still on this subject, Freitas and Hossne (2002, p. 143) consider it a challenge for CEP's to "find methods to monitor the development of research in the institution, seeking to establish mechanisms to ensure that what is in the project is really what is put into practice". It should be emphasized that by monitoring the development of research projects, the CEP is checking that the study is being carried out in accordance with the approved protocol, ensuring that scientific research is built and developed based on ethical standards and the protection of research participants.

Regarding CEP/IFPB's communication process with its main stakeholders, according to respondent C, communication takes place via the Brazil Platform, e-mail, telephone, face-to-face contact and by letter.

Respondent C informs us that communication via the Brazil Platform takes place when the CEP secretariat refuses to accept documents, when it is found that the documents submitted do not meet the minimum requirements to be validated. In this case, the researcher in charge is informed of the reasons for the return of their research protocol so that they can make adjustments. Communication via the Brazil Platform is also used when the CEP issues its substantiated opinion, in which the researcher is informed of the duly substantiated decision on their research protocol, which may be pending, approved or not approved.

According to respondent C, e-mail, telephone and face-to-face communication is used to contact researchers and committee members. Through these channels it is possible for researchers and committee members to ask questions, make requests and suggestions. CEP/IFPB uses e-mail and telephone communication to contact researchers and inform them of points relating to the analysis of their research protocols whenever necessary. For members, the Committee uses e-mail and telephone mainly to provide guidance and call meetings.

CONEP uses e-mail communication to send notices or other information of interest to the Committee. CEP, on the other hand, uses e-mail communication mainly to answer questions and request updates from CONEP, while telephone communication is basically used to obtain guidance.

According to respondent C, communication by letter is used to send reports and changes to the Committee's data to CONEP, among other things. CONEP uses this channel to send information of interest to the Committee.

It is important to note that in the process of communicating with researchers and members of the collegiate body, CEP/IFPB plays both an advisory and educational role. The guidance provided by the Committee to these audiences contributes to the construction and development of ethically responsible scientific knowledge.

With regard to the promotion of educational activities by the Committee, respondent C reports that they take place both for the institution's researchers and for the new members of the CEP collegiate body. This information is in line with CNS Resolution 466/12, which assigns research ethics committees the role of carrying out educational activities relating to questions of ethics in research involving human beings (BRASIL, 2012).

According to respondent C, "For researchers, as our institute has several campuses, we try throughout the year, when we visit the various units, to hold meetings with researchers, teachers, administrative technicians, scholarship holders and students. We inform them of the basic procedures for submitting projects to the CEP, the importance of research involving human beings, how it should be carried out ethically [...] how to register on the Brazil Platform and we also take the opportunity to show them the most common pending issues in research protocols, with the aim of minimizing them. Now this is a dynamic thing and it has to be constant, because as it is an educational institution, every semester students come and go, civil servants come and go, so this is a constant need and we intend to intensify this issue of workshops with the community, so that the research protocols to be analyzed have fewer and fewer pending issues and are approved more quickly, this is our expectation of improving training".

Considering what respondent C said, it can be seen that the promotion of educational activities is of significant importance, since it is the role of research ethics committees to promote actions that develop their educational function, resulting in a greater sensitivity of their researchers and the community in relation to ethical problems (FREITAS; HOSSNE, 1998).

According to respondent C, the promotion of educational activities for new members of the Committee usually begins with the new member being given all the documentation and legislation in force on ethics in research involving human beings. From then on, the new member follows the meetings to observe the dynamics and answer any questions. After this process, usually from the third meeting onwards, the new member begins to receive research protocols to report on, starting with the simplest ones until they are confident enough to analyze the more complex ones.

It is worth mentioning that by playing its educational role in relation to researchers and members of the collegiate body, the CEP/IFPB is encouraging ethical reflection in the scientific research carried out at the Institute, contributing to studies guided by ethical development standards and, at the same time, safeguarding the rights of the research participant.

It should also be noted that, according to respondent C, the promotion of educational activities is only aimed at researchers and new CEP members. However, these activities should also include research participants and the community in general, as well as promoting not only initial training, but also continuing education for its members (BRASIL, 2008).

With regard to the difficulties faced by the CEP/IFPB, respondent C points to issues related to the number of meetings, the training of the institution's researchers and landline telephony. With regard to the quorum of meetings, respondent C points out that "we recently had a very difficult time reaching the minimum quorum, because some of our members, for justified reasons, were unable to attend the meetings. As we have a CEP with a relatively large number of members, we need to have at least nine present and, as a result, we were often unable to deliberate on research protocols. However, because some of these members were unable to attend the meetings, they asked to leave and we replaced them and I believe that this problem has now diminished a lot because we are achieving a quorum easily. So this was a problem that we used to have and today, normally, we don't have it anymore".

Regarding the training of IFPB researchers in the field of ethics in research involving human beings, respondent C says that "Another difficulty we have is the need to better train researchers, because we understand that many research protocols are of excellent technical quality, but from an ethical point of view, they still come with some flaws that are not in accordance with what is required by Resolution 466 of 2012, so that we are reworking, analyzing, issuing pending protocols with simple things, but which we have to check. This slows down research". This information is in line with Freitas and Hossne (2002), who consider it a challenge for RECs to strengthen the promotion of educational action with researchers, even during the project preparation phase, in order to make them aware of the ethical aspects of the study and the interests and rights of the research participants.

The third difficulty noted by respondent C concerns the temporary lack of landline telephony in the CEP: "the building still doesn't have landline telephony, so we're temporarily without a landline and fax, and that's why we're using a mobile phone, which is shared with other sectors".

According to the information collected in the interview with respondent C, it can be seen that the Committee has satisfactory general operating conditions, which makes it possible for it to contribute to the construction and development of scientific knowledge at the Institute. However, it is also clear that the CEP needs to optimize some points in order to perform its activities better.

As for CEP/IFPB's trends for the coming years, respondent C points out that the Institute has been expanding a lot in recent years. Initially, the new campuses start with a small number of courses, which quickly increase, also increasing the number of research projects carried out at the institution. In this context, according to respondent C, "Some of this research involves human beings and we are going to increase the demand on our CEP and, even with the Plataforma Brasil tool, it will be impossible for the Committee to deal with all this in a short time. This will require new CEP's to be opened on the various campuses, for example we have the Joao Pessoa Campus, which is already able to have its own research ethics committee".

3.3 RESEARCH PROTOCOLS CONSIDERED BY THE IFPB RESEARCH ETHICS COMMITTEE FROM JANUARY/2010 TO DECEMBER/2014

The data inherent in the characterization of the research protocols examined by the CEP/IFPB was extracted from various types of documents, as can be seen in Table 2.

Chart 2 - Documents used to characterize the research protocols

DOCUMENTS ANALYZED	PROCEDURES ADOPTED
CEP/IFPB half-yearly reports	Verification of the activities carried out by the Committee each semester and the number of protocols examined, approved, not approved, withdrawn or archived.
Research protocols considered by CEP/IFPB	Verification of the area of knowledge, number of projects per IFPB campus or other institutions, professional category and title of the researchers responsible and number of researchers per protocol.
Consubstantiated opinions issued by CEP/IFPB	Verification of the number of protocols that received a "Pending" Consent Opinion before being "Approved".

Source: own elaboration, 2015.

The documentary data was collected from December 1, 2014 to January 30, 2015 at the CEP/IFPB facilities. The aspects relating to the research protocols examined and the substantiated opinions issued by the CEP/IFPB in 2010 and 2011 were collected using printed documents held in the Committee's archives. Aspects of these same documents, but referring to the period from 2012 to 2014, were collected from digital documents on the Brazil Platform.

From 2010 to 2014, 228 (two hundred and twenty eight) research protocols[7] were

7 The analysis did not take into account research protocols that were in a "pending" status at the end of each year, as this characteristic is transitory, given that in the following year the project acquires one of the following statuses: approved, not approved, withdrawn or archived.

examined by the CEP/IFPB, as can be seen in Graph 1. These protocols had the most diverse purposes: scientific initiation projects, monographs for undergraduate and specialization courses, master's dissertations, among others. According to Batista *et al* (2012), for a protocol to be submitted to the CEP, it doesn't matter what level the research is at, whether it's undergraduate course completion work, scientific initiation projects or any other study of academic or operational interest, it's enough that the research involves human beings.

Graph 1 - Research protocols considered by CEP/IFPB - 2010 to 2014

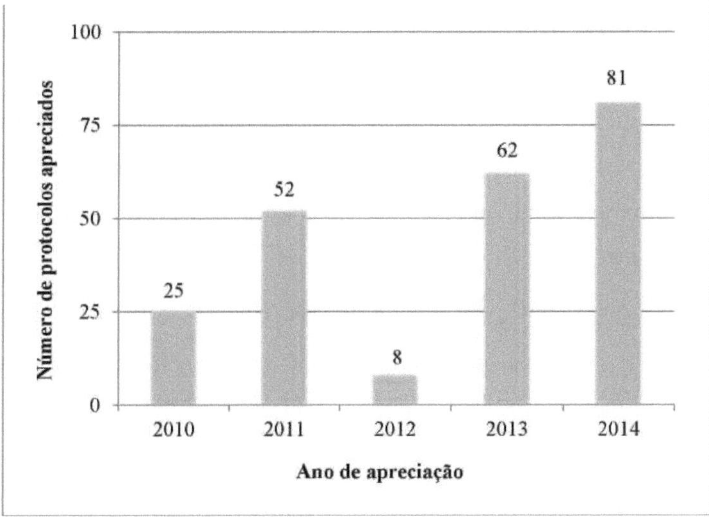

Source: own elaboration, 2015.

The significant number of research protocols assessed during the period reflects the deliberative and educational role played by the CEP/IFPB. The deliberations on the research protocols evaluated are based on the ethicality of the projects analyzed and the guidelines contained in the opinions resulting from the deliberations have an educational nature, contributing to the ethical quality of the scientific research carried out at the Institute and, at the same time, to the protection of the study participant.

It can be seen that, during the period under analysis, there was a progressive annual increase in the number of research protocols sent to the CEP for evaluation, except in 2012, when there was a significant drop.

Although CEP/IFPB was approved by CONEP in October 2009, the first research protocols submitted to the Committee date back to the beginning of the second half of 2010, and the first submission took place on June 7th of that year.

The activities carried out in 2009 were marked by planning meetings, while the first half of 2010 saw the development of educational activities with the internal community, the creation of standardized documents and the creation of the CEP website, with the aim of making information available to researchers.

Also in 2009, starting in April, the IFPB's Dean of Research, Innovation and Postgraduate Studies made it a prerequisite for enrolling in the Institute's research grant programs to submit a research project involving human beings for analysis by the CEP by the deadline for applications. However, if the project was accepted, the receipt of grants was conditional on the project's prior approval by the Research Ethics Committee. This procedure only came into force in 2010, as the Committee was only registered at the end of October 2009.

These initial actions developed by the CEP and the PRPIPG were directly responsible for the number of research protocols examined by the Committee in 2010, which corresponded to 10.96% of the total examined in the period under analysis.

In 2011, the number of research protocols examined by the CEP increased by more than 100% compared to the previous year. Some factors were decisive in this increase. The first was the dissemination of information on the existence of the CEP at the various IFPB campuses. This educational activity, developed through lectures, also sought to disseminate the importance of the Committee in research involving human beings, as well as the procedures necessary for submitting research protocols.

Another relevant factor contributing to this increase was the maintenance of the prerequisite of prior submission to the Research Ethics Committee, according to the same criteria adopted from 2010 onwards, of the projects participating in the IFPB's research grant calls. The research protocols examined by the CEP in 2011 correspond to 22.81% of the period under analysis.

In 2012 there was a significant drop in the number of protocols examined by the CEP/IFPB, down 84.62% on the previous year. The main factor behind this was a change in the process for submitting research protocols.

Since its creation, CEP/IFPB has followed a standard procedure for submitting research protocols. In this process, in order to submit a project, the researcher had to go to the institution's CEP and submit the necessary documentation. With the advent of Plataforma Brasil, CONEP, through Letter no. 327/2011/CONEP/CNS/MS, of November 18, 2011, instructed that as of 2012, CEP's should use this system to receive research protocols. For Batista *et al* (2012), the implementation of the Brazil Platform took place in January 2012 and aimed to cover the entire CEP/CONEP System.

In this sense, at the beginning of the first semester of 2012, CONEP and the Plataforma Brasil support team were asked to register the CEP/IFPB coordinator profile so that the system could be enabled for the Committee. However, this request was only answered in October of that year. As a result, CEP/IFPB spent 9 (nine) months in 2012 without carrying out any ethical analysis of research protocols, which led to a sharp drop in the number of projects assessed. The number of research protocols reviewed that year was only 3.51%, the lowest in the period under analysis.

In 2013, with the Brazil Platform already enabled for operation by CEP/IFPB, there was a resumption of the progressive increase seen in previous years. This year, a reasonable number of the research protocols examined by the Committee, approximately 34%, related to final year coursework from the Higher Course in Occupational Safety Technology at the Patos Campus, due to the wide dissemination of the CEP/IFPB, promoted by the coordination of that Course. The research protocols examined that year account for 27.19% of the period under analysis at .

In 2014, the number of research protocols examined increased by 30.65% compared to the previous year. This significant percentage is mainly due to the maintenance of the Committee's publicity work, carried out by the coordinators of the Higher Technology Course in Occupational Safety at the Patos Campus, as well as the start of publicity for the CEP/IFPB, promoted by the coordinators of the Higher Technology Course in

Commercial Management at the Guarabira Campus and the Higher Technology Course in Food at the Sousa Campus. The research protocols examined this year correspond to the highest percentage seen in the period under analysis, representing 35.53%.

3.3.1 Protocols approved, not approved, withdrawn and archived

Table 1 shows that most of the research protocols examined by the CEP/IFPB between 2010 and 2014 were approved (187 or 82.02%). Of these, 52 (27.81%) were approved in the first analysis and 135 (72.19%) received a "pending" opinion before being approved. According to CNS Resolution 466/2012 (X.3.5.b) a research protocol is considered pending "when the CEP considers it necessary to correct the protocol submitted, and requests specific revision, modification or relevant information, which must be met within a period stipulated in an operational rule" (BRASIL, 2012). It is important to note that the high number of research protocols that remained pending in the first analysis reinforces respondent C's statement that the projects submitted to the Committee are of excellent technical quality, but from an ethical point of view they need to be improved, which can be achieved by increasing the CEP's educational activities with researchers.

Among the approved research protocols, there are 2 (two) that were assessed by the CEP/IFPB as co-participants[8] . According to Resolution CNS No. 466/2012 (II.9), a co-participating institution is a "public or private organization, legally constituted and qualified, in which any of the phases or stages of the research is carried out" (BRASIL, 2012).

In the case of the 2 (two) co-participant research protocols assessed by CEP/IFPB, as the proposing institutions had CEP, they were first assessed by the research ethics

8 As far as processing is concerned, according to letter no. 0212/CONEP/CNS, a research protocol that has a co-participating institution will first be assessed by the Research Ethics Committee of the proposing institution, which is the one from which the project will be proposed, if it has a REC. Secondly, after approval by the main institution, the project will be assessed by the CEP of the co-participating institution, which can only issue an "approved" or "not approved" opinion. If the proposing institution does not have a Committee, the research protocol will be sent, via the Brazil Platform, to CONEP, which will promote the appointment of a Research Ethics Committee to assess the project, preferably the CEP of the co-participating institution, if it has a Committee. Otherwise, CONEP will forward the research protocol to another committee closer to the location of the study.

committees of the respective institutions, receiving a "pending" opinion in the first analysis and then an "approved" opinion Only after this last analysis was CEP/IFPB able to assess the 2 (two) research protocols, issuing an "approved" opinion. In this context, the two co-participant research protocols were included among the 135 (one hundred and thirty-five) that received a "pending" opinion before being approved.

Table 1 - Research protocols approved, not approved, withdrawn and archived by CEP/IFPB - 2010 to 2014

Status of protocols	Quantity	%
Approved	187	82,02
Not approved	8	3,51
Withdrawn	20	8,77
Archived	13	5,70
Total	228	100,00

Source: own elaboration, 2015.

Twenty (20) research protocols were withdrawn and, according to CNS Resolution 466/2012, a research protocol is considered withdrawn when there is a request from the researcher responsible (BRASIL, 2012).

It's important to note that until 2011, according to CNS Resolution 196/96, in addition to the aforementioned characteristic, research protocols were also considered to have been withdrawn when the researchers didn't comment on the pending issues pointed out by the committee within 60 (sixty) days (BRASIL, 1996). Since 2012, after the process of revising CNS Resolution 196/96, a withdrawn project has only been considered to be one that has been requested to be withdrawn at the request of the researcher. Research protocols in which the researchers did not respond to the pending issues listed by the CEP within 60 (sixty) days are now called archived. CNS Resolution 466/2012, which revoked Resolution 196/96, maintained this same guideline, but the time limit within which the researcher must express their opinion on the pending issues listed, instead of 60 (sixty) days, was defined in an operational rule[9]

9 Operational Standard 01/2013 stipulated a deadline of 30 days for the researcher responsible to respond to

. In this context, protocols with archived status have only been accounted for since 2012.

Unapproved research protocols represent the lowest percentage (3.51%). This figure is a reflection of some of the educational actions carried out by the CEP, mainly lectures given at the institution's various campuses. The CEP/IFPB also has a telephone number, an e-mail address and a reception room, through which researchers can find an open channel for guidance on how to carry out research in accordance with ethical standards. Also through these channels, the researcher can seek guidance on any pending issues that have been pointed out in their research protocol. This allows them to adjust the project before submitting it for consideration again, which contributes to the ethical quality of the research to be carried out.

3.3.2 Broad areas of knowledge of the protocols examined

With regard to the major areas of knowledge (Table 2), it was noted that the research protocols examined by the CEP/IFPB belonged to various major areas of knowledge, with a predominance for the Human Sciences, Applied Social Sciences and Health Sciences, which together account for 60.52% of the projects examined. This heterogeneity of areas of knowledge reinforces the statement made by respondent A, who made it clear during the interview that research ethics committees do not only analyze projects in the Health Sciences area. At the same time, it also corroborates Freitas and Hossne's (1998, p. 199) statement that "all research involving human beings must be subjected to ethical reflection in order to ensure respect for the identity, integrity and dignity of the human person and the practice of solidarity and social justice". It is also worth noting that CNS Resolution 466/2012 states that all research involving human beings, regardless of the area of knowledge, must be submitted to the CEP/CONEP System, made up of research ethics committees and the National Research Ethics Commission (BRASIL, 2012).

---

the pending issues listed in the opinion issued by the Research Ethics Committee via the Brazil Platform. From 2012 until the publication of Operational Standard 01/2013 (30/09/2013), the CEP/IFPB stipulated a period of 90 days for the researcher responsible to respond to the pending issues listed in the opinion issued by the CEP.

Table 2 - Broad areas of knowledge of research projects

Large areas	Quantity	%
Exact and Earth Sciences	14	6,14
Biological Sciences	1	0,44
Engineering	10	4,39
Health Sciences	42	18,42
Agricultural Sciences	19	8,34
Applied Social Sciences	48	21,05
Humanities	48	21,05
Linguistics, Literature and Arts	5	2,19
Others	12	5,26
More than one large area	29	12,72
Total	228	100,00

Source: own elaboration, 2015.

It is important to note that, in 29 (twenty-nine) of the research protocols analyzed, the researchers responsible for their projects fell into more than one major area of knowledge: 8 (Applied Social Sciences/Human Sciences), 5 (Engineering/Health Sciences), 2 (Biological Sciences/Engineering/Health Sciences), 2 (Engineering/Human Sciences/Workplace Safety), 2 (Engineering/Applied Social Sciences), 1 (Human Sciences/Linguistics, Letters and Arts), 1 (Applied Social Sciences/Linguistics, Letras e Artes), 1 (Biological Sciences / Health Sciences), 1 (Exact and Earth Sciences / Health Sciences), 1 (Biological Sciences / Health Sciences / Multidisciplinary), 1 (Exact and Earth Sciences / Applied Social Sciences / Human Sciences), 1 (Applied Social Sciences / Human Sciences / Linguistics, Letters and Arts), 1 (Engineering / Health Sciences / Occupational Safety), 1 (Engineering / Applied Social Sciences / Water Management) and 1 (Engineering / Occupational Safety / Engineering / Ergonomics).

3.3.3 Campus of origin of the protocols examined

In terms of the campus from which the research protocols originated (Table 3), it was found that the vast majority of the projects assessed by the CEP/IFPB came from the Joao Pessoa Campus, representing 35.53% of the total assessed during the period under analysis. Some factors contribute to this configuration.

The Joao Pessoa Campus is the oldest in the IFPB, currently offering 1 (one) *stricto sensu* postgraduate course, 2 (two) *lato sensu* postgraduate courses, 13 (thirteen) higher education courses and 8 (eight) technical courses, with a strong commitment to research activities.

The annual average number of research protocols from the Joao Pessoa Campus that were examined by the Committee during the period under analysis is approximately 16 (sixteen) projects. This significant number of research protocols from the Joao Pessoa Campus, as reported by respondent C in the interview, points to a strong trend towards the creation of a research ethics committee on this campus. CONEP currently recommends that research ethics committees examine at least 12 (twelve) research protocols a year.

Table 3 - Campus of origin of research protocols

Campus	Number of projects
Cabedelo	9
Cajazeiras	6
Campina Grande	14
Guarabira	8
Joao Pessoa	81
Monteiro	5
Patos	50
Picui	14
Princess Isabel	0
Rectorate	8
Sousa	23
Other institutions	9

No institution	1
Total	228

Source: own elaboration, 2015.

It was found that the Princesa Isabel Campus had no protocols appraised during the period under analysis. This fact indicates that the CEP/IFPB should develop educational activities with researchers at that unit, with the aim of sensitizing them to the importance of submitting projects involving human beings to the institution's CEP, thus contributing to the construction and development of scientific knowledge based on ethical reflection at that campus.

On other campuses, such as Cabedelo, Cajazeiras and Monteiro, the CEP/IFPB's training actions should be reinforced, given the low number of protocols examined. At the Rectory and the Guarabira Campus, the low number of research protocols coming from those units is justifiable. The Rectory, due to its administrative nature, does not carry out many research activities. Meanwhile, the Guarabira Campus was inaugurated recently, in 2011. Therefore, research activities on this campus are still at an early stage of development. The research protocols for this campus began to be submitted to the CEP/IFPB at in 2014.

We also noticed that 9 (nine) of the research protocols analyzed belonged to other institutions and 1 (one) did not have a proposing institution. This occurs when the researcher responsible, when filling in the research protocol on the Brazil Platform, in the proposing institution field, indicates an institution that does not have a research ethics committee or when the researcher responsible informs that he does not have a proposing institution. Research protocols with these characteristics will be sent to CONEP. In this case, according to Resolution 466/2012, "in the absence of a CEP at the proposing institution or in the case of a researcher with no institutional ties, CONEP will be responsible for appointing a CEP to analyze the research from among those best able to monitor it" (BRASIL, 2012). This shows that the 10 (ten) research protocols not belonging to IFPB campuses were sent to the institution's CEP through CONEP.

3.3.4 Professional category and degree of the researchers responsible for the research protocols examined

With regard to the professional category of the researchers responsible for the research protocols analyzed, it was found that 198 (86.85%) were IFPB professors and only 20 (8.77%) were IFPB administrative technicians. The professional category of 10 (4.38%) researchers who did not belong to the IFPB staff was not identified.

The significant number of research protocols examined by the CEP/IFPB and submitted by teachers at the institution is a determining factor in the link between teaching and research activities. *On the other hand, the* small number of research protocols examined by administrative staff are mainly projects for the development of monographs for postgraduate courses, as well as for the supervision of research projects.

With regard to the qualifications of the researchers responsible for the research protocols (Graph 2), it was found that of the 228 (two hundred and twenty-eight) projects examined, 120 (one hundred and twenty) researchers had a master's degree, 63 (sixty-three) had a doctorate, 38 (thirty-eight) had a specialization, 6 (six) had a bachelor's degree and 1 (one) had a high school degree. It is worth noting that the researcher who only had a high school degree stated that he had completed higher education, but that his Lattes curriculum only contained a degree in progress. This fact was noted by the CEP/IFPB during the appraisal of the research protocol, which issued a "not approved" opinion, given that to be a researcher in charge you need to have at least completed higher education.

Graph 2 - Title of researchers responsible for research protocols assessed by CEP/IFPB - 2010 to 2014

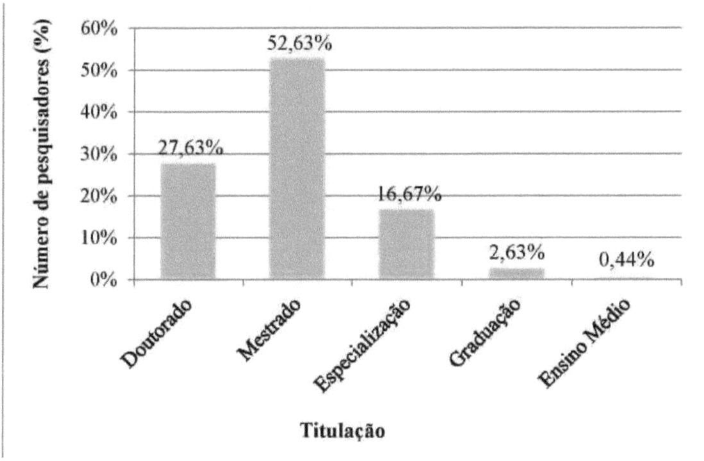

Source: own elaboration, 2015.

The large number of researchers with master's degrees and doctorates (80.26%) is a reflection of the qualification policy for teachers and administrative technicians, which is generally present in federal institutes. When they qualify, teachers are entitled to the Retribution for Titling. Administrative technicians, on the other hand, are entitled to the Qualification Incentive and, in an effort to further solidify this strategy, the IFPB has also entered into partnerships with other institutions to offer its employees *stricto sensu* postgraduate courses.

3.3.5 Number of researchers per protocol

With regard to the number of researchers per protocol, it was found that the 228 (two hundred and twenty eight) research projects examined by the CEP/IFPB were submitted by 118 (one hundred and eighteen) researchers, as can be seen in Table 4.

The majority of the research protocols examined by the Committee belonged to researchers who submitted just one (1) project, representing 34.21% of the research protocols examined during the period under analysis.

Table 4 - Number of researchers per research protocol examined by the IFPB REC - 2010 to 2014

Research protocols submitted by researcher	Number of researchers	Total number of research protocols examined

1	78	78
2	19	38
3	6	18
4	5	20
5	5	25
Above 5	5	49
Total	118	228

Source: own elaboration, 2015.

It is interesting to mention that as the number of research protocols submitted per researcher increases, the number of researchers decreases, except after 4 (four) protocols, where the number of researchers becomes constant.

4 FINAL CONSIDERATIONS

The main objective of this book was to analyze the importance of the Research Ethics Committee in the construction and development of scientific knowledge at IFPB. It was found that the CEP/IFPB was the brainchild of a researcher at the Institution, who recognized that the time was right to invest in the scientific research carried out at the Institute. This idea was combined with three other factors that provided a favorable context for the creation of the CEP/IFPB: expansion of the Institute and, consequently, the need to encourage ethical reflection in the research carried out; requirements for recognition of courses by INEP and, finally, the guidelines contained in CNS Resolution No. 196/96 regarding the creation of research ethics committees in institutions that carry out studies involving human beings.

With regard to the general operating conditions, it was found that the CEP/IFPB has satisfactory conditions for promoting the ethical review of research involving human beings, although some points need to be improved in terms of furnishings, monitoring the development of research projects and promoting educational activities.

With regard to the trends of the CEP/IFPB, it was found that due to the growth of the institution and, consequently, the increase in the number of research projects carried out, it will be necessary to create new research ethics committees, with the aim of contributing to the ethical quality of the research carried out at the Institute and, consequently, to greater protection for the study participant.

With regard to research protocols, it was possible to verify that CEP/IFPB assessed 228 (two hundred and twenty eight) between 2010 and 2014 and that each year there was a gradual increase in the number of research protocols assessed, with the exception of 2012, due to operational problems. The significant number of protocols examined shows that the CEP/IFPB has been contributing to and encouraging the development of research guided by ethical standards at the Institute.

It was also possible to observe that the majority of the 228 (two hundred and twenty-eight) protocols examined were approved (187) and, of these, 135 received a "pending" opinion before approval. This fact points to the need for CEP/IFPB to increase its educational activities with researchers, with a view to improving the development of research protocols within ethical standards.

It was also found that the CEP/IFPB considered research protocols in all areas of knowledge, with a predominance for Applied Social Sciences, Human Sciences and Health Sciences. This points to the fact that ethical reflection must be present in all research involving human beings, regardless of their area of knowledge.

As for the origin of the research protocols examined, the data showed that the vast majority came from the Joao Pessoa and Patos campuses. The data obtained suggests the creation of a research ethics committee at the Joao Pessoa Campus and the reinforcement of educational activities at the campuses with a low number of protocols examined.

With regard to the professional category and degree of the researchers responsible for the research protocols analyzed, it was found that the majority are IFPB professors, and a small proportion are administrative technicians from the Institute and professionals from other institutions.

With regard to the number of researchers per protocol, the data collected showed that the 228 (two hundred and twenty-eight) protocols examined by the CEP/IFPB were submitted by only 118 (one hundred and eighteen) researchers and that the vast majority (78) submitted only 1 (one) research protocol.

In view of the above, it can be seen that the specific objectives outlined made it possible to achieve the central objective of this work. The development of this work made it possible to conclude that the CEP/IFPB plays an advisory, deliberative and educational role in the exercise of its functions, being of fundamental importance in the construction and development of scientific knowledge at the Institute, fostering ethical reflection in the scientific research carried out and contributing to the development of studies guided by ethical standards and respect for the research participant.

With a view to continuing and deepening work on the IFPB Research Ethics Committee, the following are recommendations for future work:

- To broaden the scope of this book, seeking to find out the profile of current and former members of the CEP/IFPB;
- Develop work aimed at understanding the perception of IFPB researchers about the role of the institutional CEP;
- Evaluate the usability of the Brazil Platform among IFPB researchers.

REFERENCES

ARAÙJO, Lais Zàu Serpa de. A brief history of bioethics: from research ethics to bioethics. In: REGO, Sérgio; PALACIOS, Marisa (Org.). **Research Ethics Committees:** theory and practice. Rio de Janeiro: Editora Fiocruz, 2012. chap. 3, p. 71-84.

. Ethical aspects of scientific research. **Pesquisa Odontológica Brasileira**, Sao Paulo, v. 17, supl. 1, 2003. Available at:< http://www.scielo.br/ scielo.php?script=sci_arttext&pid=S1517-74912003000500009&lng=en&nrm=iso>. Accessed on: February 3, 2015.

AZEVEDO, Maria Alice da Silva. Origins of Bioethics. **Nascer e Crescer**, Porto, v. 19, n. 4, 2010. Available at: <http://www.scielo.gpeari.mctes.pt/scielo.php?script= sci_arttext&pid=S0872-07542010000400005&lng=en&nrm=iso>. Accessed on: 05 Nov. 2013.

BATISTA, Kàtia Torres *et al*. The role of research ethics committees. **Revista Brasileira Cirurgia Plàstica**, Sao Paulo, v. 27, n. 1, 2012. Available at:< http:// www.scielo.br/scielo.php?script=sci_arttext&pid=S1983-51752012000100025&lng= en&nrm=iso>. Accessed on: January 13, 2014.

BOCCATO, Marlene. The importance of bioethics. Available at:< http://blog.cca. ufscar.br/lamam/files/2010/07/bioetica_21.pdf>. Accessed on: October 14, 2013.

BRAZIL. Ministry of Health. National Health Council. **Operational Manual for Research Ethics Committees.** Brasilia: Ministry of Health, 2008.

. Ministry of Health. National Health Council. **Operational Standard 001/2013.** Provides for the organization and functioning of the CEP/CONEP System, and for the procedures for submitting, evaluating and monitoring research and development involving human beings in Brazil, under the terms of item 5, of Chapter XIII, of CNS Resolution No. 466 of 12 December 2012. Available at: <http://conselho.saude.gov.br/web_comissoes/conep/aquivos/CNS%20%20Norma% 20Operacional%20001%20-%20conep%20finalizada%2030-09.pdf>. Accessed on:

January 14, 2014.

. Ministry of Health. National Health Council. **Resolution 001, of June 13, 1988.** Approves health research norms. Available at:< http:// conselho.saude.gov.br/resolucoes/1988/Reso01.doc>. Accessed on: January 13, 2014.

. Ministry of Health. National Health Council. **Resolution No. 196, of October 10, 1996.** Approves the guidelines and regulatory standards for research involving human beings. Available at:< http://conselho.saude.gov.br /web_comissoes/conep/aquivos/resolucoes/23_out_versao_final_196_ENCEP2012.p df>. Accessed on: 14 Jan. 2014.

. Ministry of Health. National Health Council. **Resolution No. 466, of December 12, 2012.** Approves the guidelines and regulatory standards for research involving human beings. Available at:< http://conselho.saude.gov.br /resolucoes/2012/Reso466.pdf>. Accessed on: January 14, 2014.

. Ministry of Health. National Health Council. National Commission for Ethics in Research. Map of CEPs 2014. Available at:< http://conselho.saude.gov.br/ web_comissoes/conep/aquivos/MAPA_CEP_ATUALIZADO_2014.jpg>. Accessed on: 27 Nov. 2014.

CARBONIERI, Fernando. Nazi Medical Experiments. Available at:< http:// academiamedica.com.br/experimentos-medicos-nazistas/>. Accessed on: October 8, 2013.

CARVALHO, Fernanda Maria Ferreira; PESSINI, Léo; CAMPOS JUNIOR, Oswaldo. Reflections on environmental bioethics. Available at: <http://www.unioeste. br/cursos/cascavel/posmicrobiologia/arq/Reflexoes_sobre_Bioetica_Ambiental_carva lho_2006.pdf>. Accessed on: December 10, 2013.

CASCAIS, António Fernando. Human experimentation and the crisis of self-regulation in biomedicine. **Anâlise Social**, Lisbon, n. 181, 2006. Available at: <http://www. scielo.gpeari.mctes.pt/scielo.php?script=sci_arttext&pid=S0003-257320060004000 03&lng=en&nrm=iso>. Accessed on: 06 Nov. 2013.

COSTA, Sérgio. The challenge of research ethics and bioethics. In: DINIZ, Débora *et al* (org.). **Ethics in research:** global themes. Editora UNB, 2008. P. 25-52.

DALL'AGNOL, Darlei. Philosophy and bioethics in the Brazilian public debate. Available at: <http://www.ifch.unicamp.br/ojs/index.php/ideias/article/view/860/644>. Accessed on: November 13, 2013.

DEJEANNE, Solange. The foundations of bioethics and principialist theory. Available at: <http://sites.unifra.br/Portals/1/ARTIGOS/nro_06/SOLANGE.pdf>. Accessed on: 06 Nov. 2013.

DINIZ, Débora; GUILHEM, Dirce. Ethics in research in Brazil. In: DINIZ, Débora; GUILHEM, Dirce; SCHÜKLENK, Udo (Eds.). **Ethics in research:** training experience in South African countries. Brasilia: Letras Livres, Editora UnB, 2005.p. 11-28.

DINIZ, Débora; CORRÊA, Marilena. Declaration of Helsinki: relativism and vulnerability. **Cadernos de Saùde Pùblica**, Rio de Janeiro, v. 17, n. 3, 2001. Available at: <http://www.scielo.br/scielo.php?script=sci_arttext&pid=S0102-311X2001000300022&lng=en&nrm=iso>. Accessed on: October 10, 2013.

FREITAS, Corina Bontempo D.; HOSSNE, William Saad. Research with human beings. In: COSTA, Sérgio Ibiapina Ferreira; GARRAFA, Volnei; OSELKA, Gabriel (Org.). **Iniciaçâo à Bioética**. Brasilia: Federal Council of Medicine, 1998. p. 193-204.

. The role of research ethics committees in protecting human beings. Available at:< http://revistabioetica.cfm.org.br/index.php/revista_bioetica/article /view/218/219>. Accessed on: February 3, 2015.

FUENTES, Lygia Aride. Reflections on bioethics: dialoguing with C. G. Jung and Peter Singer. Available at:< http://www.ufrrj.br/seminariopsi/2011/boletim2011-1/boletim.pdf#page=111>. Accessed on: December 19, 2013.

GARRAFA, Volnei. A brief history of the genesis and consolidation of bioethics.

Available at:< http://www.univesp.ensinosuperior.sp.gov.br/preunivesp/801/breve-hist-rico-sobre-a-g-nese-e-a-consolida-o-da-bio-tica.html>. Accessed on: 31. Oct. 2013.

. Introducing bioethics. Available at: <http://www.publicacoes academicas.uniceub.br/index.php/face/article/viewFile/118/102>. Accessed on: 06 Nov. 2013.

. Bioethical radiography of a country - Brazil. Available at: <http://www. redalyc.org/articulo.oa?id=55460115>. Accessed on: November 12, 2013.

GOLDIM, José Roberto. Bioethics: origins and complexity. Available at: <http://www.bioetica.ufrgs.br/complex.pdf>. Accessed on: October 31, 2013.

. The Tuskegee Case: when science becomes ethically inappropriate. Available at:< http://www.ufrgs.br/bioetica/tueke2.htm>. Accessed on: October 7, 2013.

GUERRA, Andréa Trevas Maciel. From the Nazi holocaust to the new eugenics in the 21st century. **Ciência e Cultura,** Sao Paulo, v. 58, n. 1, 2006. Available at: <http://ciencia ecultura.bvs.br/scielo.php?pid=s0009-67252006000100002&script=sci_arttext>.

Accessed on: 08 Oct. 2013.

HARDY, Ellen *et al.* Research ethics committees: adaptation to Resolution 196/96. **Revista da Associaçâo Mèdica Brasileira**, Sao Paulo, v. 50, n. 4, 2004. Available at: <http://www.scielo.br/scielo.php?script=sci_arttext&pid=S0104-423020040004 00040&lng=en&nrm=iso>. Accessed on: Jan. 14, 2014.

HOSSNE, William Saad *et al.* Bioethics at 40: reflections from a time of uncertainty. Available at:< http://www.saocamilo-sp.br/pdf/bioethikos/76/130a 143.pdf> Accessed on: Nov. 11, 2013.

KIPPER, José Délio. A brief history of research ethics. **Revista da AMRIGS,** Porto Alegre, v. 54, n. 2, 2010. Available at:< http://www.amrigs.com.br/revista/ 54-02/20-643_breve_historia.pdf>. Accessed on: October 4, 2013.

KOTTOW, Miguel. History of ethics in research with human beings. In: DINIZ,

Débora *et al* (org.). **Ética em pesquisa:** temas globais. Editora UNB, 2008. P. 53-86.

LAUREANO, Màrcia Ferrér Machado. Evaluation of continuous monitoring in the adherence of volunteers to investigational product in randomized clinical trials. 2013. 127 f. Dissertation (Master's in Nursing) - Postgraduate Program in Nursing, University of Brasilia - UNB, Brasilia, DF, 2013.

MARQUES, Marilia Bernardes. Bioethics in Brazilian public policy. Available at: <http://revistabioetica.cfm.org.br/index.php/revista_bioetica/article/view/408/ 371>. Accessed on: November 18, 2013.

MARQUES FILHO, José. Ethics in research: ten years of CNS Resolution 196/96. **Revista Brasileira de Reumatologia**, Sao Paulo, v. 47, n. 1, 2007. Available at: <http://www.scielo.br/scielo.php?script=sci_arttext&pid=S0482-500420070001000 02&lng=en&nrm=iso>. Accessed on: 19 nov. 2013.

MARTINS, Herminio. Tanatocratic biotechnology. **Novos estudos - CEBRAP**, Sao Paulo, n. 74, 2006. Available at: <http://www.scielo.br/scielo.php?pid=S0101-330 02006000100015&script=sci_arttext>. Accessed on: October 7, 2013.

MINOSSI, José Guilherme. Informed consent: What is its real value in medical practice? **Revista do Colégio Brasileiro de Cirurgioes**, Rio de Janeiro, v.

38, n. 3, 2011. Available at: <http://www.scielo.br/scielo.php?script=sci_arttext& pid=S0100-69912011000300011&lng=en&nrm=iso>. Accessed on: October 4, 2013.

NOVAES, Maria Rita C. G.; GUILHEM, Dirce; LOLAS, Fernando. Ten years of experience of the Research Ethics Committee of the Health Department of the Federal District, Brazil. **Acta bioethica**, Santiago, v. 14, n. 2, 2008. Available at: <http:// www.scielo.cl/scielo.php?script=sci_arttext&pid=S1726-569X2008000200008&lng

=en&nrm=iso>. Accessed on: 19 Nov. 2013.

OLIVEIRA, Arthur Henrique de. Bioethics and religious conceptions. Available at: <http://periodicos.uniso.br/ojs/index.php?journal=reu&page=article&op=view&path[ ]=1491&path[]=1458>. Accessed on: Dec. 28, 2013.

OLIVEIRA, Laura de. Human rights and memory: the debate on bioethics in the second half of the 20th century. Available at: <https://portais.ufg.br/uploads/113/ original_27_LauraDeOliveira_DiretosHumanosEMemoria.pdf>. Accessed on: November 13, 2013.

PESSINI, Leo; BARCHIFONTAINE, Christian de Paul de. **Problemas atuais** de **bioética.** Sao Paulo: Loyola, 2007.

. A radiography of bioethics in Brazil: pioneers, educational and institutional programs and perspectives. In: PESSINI, Leo; BARCHIFONTAINE, Christian de Paul de (Org.). **Bioethics in Ibero-America** - history and perspectives. Sao Paulo: Loyola, 2007.ch. 6, p. 99-122.

PESSINI, Leo; HOSSNE, William Saad. Bioethics in Brazil: a decade of achievements (2002-2012). Available at: <http://www.saocamilo-sp.br/pdf/bioethikos/ 98/editorial-en.pdf>. Accessed on: November 20, 2013.

READING, Màrio. E-book: **Nostradamus and the third antichrist:** Napoleon, Hitler and the one yet to come**.** Translated by: Editora Pensamento. Sao Paulo: Pensamento, 2013.

VIEIRA, Sonia. Ethics and methodology in medical research. **Revista Brasileira de Saùde Materno Infantil**, Recife, v. 5, n. 2, 2005. Available at: <http://www.

scielo.br/scielo.php?script=sci_arttext&pid=S1519-38292005000200013&lng= en&nrm=iso>. Accessed on: 08 Oct. 2013.

VIEIRA, Sonia; HOSSNE, William Saad. Experimentation with human beings: ethical aspects. Available at:< http://www2.ufpel.edu.br/medicina/bioetica/cap9_ experimentacao_comhumanos_segreecohen.pdf>. Accessed on: Feb. 12, 2014.

VRETTOS, Theodore. **Alexandria:** City of Western Thought. Translated by Briggite Klein. São Paulo: Odysseus Editora, 2005.

MIX
Papier aus verantwortungsvollen Quellen
Paper from responsible sources
FSC® C105338

Printed by Books on Demand GmbH, Norderstedt / Germany